Pinol : Poems

by Sayra Pinto

Cover picture detail from "The Recipe for Rebirth: Cacao as Fish in the Mythology and Symbolism of the Ancient Maya" by Michael J. Grofe, Ph.D., Department of Native American Studies at the University of California at Davis, 9/23/2007. Colored by Sophia P. Oxendine, age 11.

Pinol : Poems

Copyright © 2012 by Sayra Pinto

All rights reserved. No part of this book may be reproduced or transmitted in any form or by any means without written permission of the author.

ISBN-10: 0985315105
ISBN-13: 978-0-9853151-0-8

Published by:
Shabda Press
Pasadena, CA 91107

*For Tata,
so you know that your kindness saved me.*

Acknowledgments

First and foremost, I thank all the forces that have come before us to surrender to us this magnificent moment. In my case, the unwritten and unknown stories of survival, of choosing to live full lives, of daring to dream the unthinkable of the women and men in my family. Ours is a story of constant defiance of the barriers that would hold us hostage. From this story, girls have emerged into women, and boys into men, who are all throughout the country and in Honduras linked by what some call a stubborn streak, and others a gift. I am fortunate to be one heiress, among many, to this lineage.

I would like to thank Elena Georgiou, Kenny Fries, and Bhanu Kapil for being such excellent advisors while I was at Goddard. Their steady guidance, and fierceness on my behalf, drove me to write an initial and then several drafts of Pinol : Poems.

Thank you Teresa Mei Chuc for showing such care for this collection of poems. Only someone who travels in the same energies as another can comprehend the depth that is present in a fellow traveler's writing.

Kristin Wilson encouraged me to pursue the MFA at Goddard, which led to the creation of this book. Thank you for sharing so many days of angst along the long birth process for this collection. Thank you for having such faith in me all along the way.

Nicole Oxendine. You breathed life into this project in every way imaginable. *Pinol* bears the imprint of your caring, tender, and thorough presence in its spirit, its structure, and its aesthetic essence.

Eleguá may you move the boulders
between me and my intention.
Eleguá of the roads and the keys,
of the reds and blacks
striping my feet.

Eleguá, road warrior!
Be here with me.
Be here with me.

Eleguá, Niñito de Atocha,
play with me.
Bi wiz mi.
Breik mi daun.
Meik mi uan.

Table of Contents

🐚 1

● 7

● ● 17

● ● ● 25

● ● ● ● 35

▬▬▬▬ 47

When the sense strikes
there are no words to name it.
But there used to be.

I speak the words spoken by lords and serfs,
conquistadores,
knights and judges,
kings and queens,
Puritans, Protestants and generals; monks,
immigrants with birthright citizenship,
the indentured;
the slaves;
some Chinese;
some brazeros;
some Somalis
the Bosnians and Serbs;
some Sudanese;
some Vietnamese;
some Laotian, Cambodian;
the Afrikaans.

I make do with this language;
conscious of the explosives:
of those guttural concoctions
proceeding toward me in time from who knows where
to convey a meaning long ago removed by another.
These words populate me
like small-poxed blankets on unsuspecting red skins.
Their remnants bury themselves deep in your skin cells
and play tricks on you
until they kill you.

My skin hurts.
Oh the burning books, the burning words,
the ancient sounds from *balancán*.[i]

I don't care what you think, or if you understand.
I just need to name that there are moments when my skin hurts.

Twins fall from the tree and live.
They walk on the Earth.
She gives birth through her red mouth.

Snakes come out of her head before she dies.
Rivers of blood make the rivers clear.
Her body lines the top of the Earth.

She creeps into the lining of our nails when we walk barefoot.
She is everywhere still, wrapping herself
on our skins over and over again.

Coatlicué lives in the snakes in our backs.
We are her children.

Her brother Kukulcán
swims in the skies.
He looks down on us and smiles.

We writhe in the space between them.

We must have been born in the morning.
It is hard to fathom
a fledgling hairless being
groveling its way into the light
through snow.

We must have been under the ground
nesting
like snakes,
writhing bodies
intertwined
keeping each other warm.

It makes sense for us to come from there;
and go back to balancán.

The First Light was within us
and the first nothingness without.
And the first nothingness
was right outside our skins.
And inside our skins glowed the first sun.

Colón called me Honduras,
depths of the Caribbean,
400 and 70 years
before I came home.

From the West, from the Vortex,
Mami ran away.
To the North, where all dreams fly.

In the North, a mighty place;
a company of
Babel, Indian faces rot.

In the North, a place for all.
The company falls.
Love is born from hurricanes.

In the North, a tale of love.
Seven hard labors.
Don Mayorga, wretched man.

In the North, a heart broke.
Mami refused to walk.
And the children raised themselves.

Y los niños alcanzan
ser varones y
hembras, llenos de agua.
Los varones y hembras
fluyen con el río
Chamelecón y abarcan.[ii]

In the West, a vortex. Ruby
went to the sunset.
Se fue a esperarme.[iii]

And as she waited she read.
She walked cobblestones.
Cassiopeia spoke to her.

Of virgin womb, a birth and the
life that followed still teems with longing.

●

•

The day I was born, Tata rose and went to work in white. I made her clothes blood red. She handed me to the nuns who made sure I received touch and Infamil feedings. Old ladies gathered around and marveled at my jaundiced body and bald head.

They wrapped me in tobacco leaves left wide and long until I was brown. Three months later, I left the mountain range and went to the fertile slaving valley. In the valley, a house of cement blocks and zinc roof plates, yellow and maroon.

In the house, four of us who were left to live into the dawn; in the wake of other lived lives. Like the kings of old, walking up the stairs to the place where their blood would run.

•

One step, a fall into space
then ground. Thick blood
overflowing eyes.

The hawk tries to eat the chick.
Angry hen momma,
trips and falls on the poor baby.

á é í ó ú tongue moves
in all directions
inside open mouth.

I sway hugging the tree branch.
Eyes closed above the
house and the mountains' steady rise.

●

In front of the cement house,
a game of stick ball.
I refuse to lose. I win.

I am in the kitchen and my
aunt says, "Learn to wash dishes to find
a good husband."

On a stool, I reach the sink,
look down and see
the dishes.
I throw them on the floor.

●

I walk behind the house and
suck on hibiscus blooms.

Carlos wears a big red cape.
He is on the roof.
He falls on me and the ground.

I sway on the branch.
Avocados grow.
I fall asleep hanging there.

Mami sits on the porch all
day long. Her feet hang
and swell. They hurt all night long.

●

Slits of the *persianas*[iv]
reveal a big blue
mask. *Yankunú*, days of dance.

Every other day Black folks
walk barefoot, ashes and dust—
the colors of their skin.

A maid says, "You are all
a bunch of light skinned Indios.
I tell you because you already know."

●

The neighbor calls me away
from stick ball in front
of the house.

While playing with my brother
and his buddy I say:

"They get on top of each other.
They rub against you.
Like this, can you believe it?

Amado showed me."

●

My grandmother would have us park her wheelchair
on the front porch of our house every morning.
Cement flowerbeds surrounded her.

She wore a yellow house dress.
Around her yellow, red and pink flowers
whose name I was too little to know.
There is a picture someplace.

From her post, she watched the people
going by between the two cement posts marking
the beginning and the end of the fence.
From time to time people would come.
They walked up to the wrought iron gate
and would lift and drop a lever to let us know they were there.
"Bang, bang, bang."

When we let them in, they would sit with grandma.
Someone made coffee and they chatted.
Inside the house I sneaked peeks through the windows.
I was not supposed to peek through the windows.
I did anyway.
I watched the men put their straw hats on their thighs, their
    backs straight,
looking at my grandmother while she told them things I could
    not hear.

I never wondered who these people were. Or why they would
    come visit.
They never came inside the house, nor did we invite them in.

Much later, through a story, I understood.

Grandma, when she still walked, cooking frantically before sunrise
in waist high waters. Men waiting eagerly outside her kitchen
before they peopled the strike lines on the plantation.

•

Beyond the house:
the avocados, the fence and
the dirt road: a school.

In the school: a woman dressed
in black sings and plays
a guitar. I sing. She leaves.

A yard full of rides.
The broken swing sways.
Green grass and trees become friends.

A drawer full
of teaching tools: paddles, inner tubes, rulers and some chalk.
I speak no more.

In the yard, at the school:
a pile of corn kernels,
bloody knees and narrowed eyes.

The river runs brown and black.

●

I am in the warm waves and
cannot see. My eyes
burn. I feel only the sand.

● ●

Lychees hang in bunches, all
for my pleasure. I
feast on the thick blue hammock.

• •

She said your mama was sad and crying.
That the doctor came to your house.
The neighbor said you were not speaking.

I saw you later, limping down the road.
Years after I jumped on a plane past the border,
You looked the other way and so did I.

Too much to be said about what floats in the *Río Grande*.
Too little can be said about the journey that brings us there.

Through the endless *milpas*ᵛ for innumerable baked tortillas
they call Doritos, or chips, or something other than what reminds
    them of us,
you ran like hell for the edge between your dream and my life.

And your ancestors must have gotten distracted, maybe.
You saw the edge of the sun above the horizon
and fell into night.

• •

From the hulls,
men in green
with incomprehensible killing things.
Long ones,
little ones,
round ones,
four-legged ones,
thin and thick ones.

They set up places where they would not be seen
but we knew they were there and we found them.
They left a mark upon departure in our skins.

• •

On the way back from Tegucigalpa,
my brother puked on me.
We got our visas that day.

One morning, we got on
a plane. Mami looked on.
Yellow robe with the flowers.

One morning, in school in New
Orleans, I walked to
the Mississippi in awe.

One morning on a plane for
Honduras, Mami
on the other side, dead.

● ●

I am child of water and
rain; of heat rising
from concrete earth in summer.

I walk through cornfields into
a river. There I
lay still until I am found.

The white hand lifts me and makes
me run through the air
into a cloud.

There I can see all the roads
and the little white
cars with the lights on the top.

There are a lot of them there
where you are living.
There are lots of us in them.

They move on the roads to the
big houses where they
put us and from where we don't come out.

• •

I sit on my suitcase on
the sidewalk in front of mother's house.
A car comes to get me home.

Home on Elysian Fields is
empty. I make friends
with the trees and the sky.

Groping hands of the deacon
while he pretended
to teach me how to drive.

A tree saved me from his
fingers. The car wreck
claimed his teeth and my desire.

• •

On Elysian Fields,
a bird is hit by
a car. It dies in my hands.

On Congo Square I learn of
dancing in the thick
of the surged black/brown river.

In St. Peter and Paul, I
learn to read and write again.
The Hobbit freed me.

• • •

There is a child someplace
that came out of my birth mother's other girl-child's womb.

There are children someplace
that came through women who shared their wombs someplace
with the boy my birth mother birthed someplace.

There are my grandma's children someplace.
Her children's children someplace.
There are her children's children's children someplace.

There are her cheating husband's other children someplace.
The cheating husband's other children's children someplace.
The cheating husband's other children's children's children
    someplace.
My grandma's sisters' children are someplace I don't know.

The cheating husband's child Tio Isaías speeding someplace
on the Lake Pontchartrain Causeway.
A crushing weight on his chest. Then, nothing more.
He is someplace on the Lake Pontchartrain Causeway.

My grandma's sister's child's child, my cousin Vito is someplace
hopefully with the man he always wanted.
His child was no-place when his mother got chickenpox in the
    first trimester.
I named him Gabriel Josué and he is someplace.

Someplace there is a woman who raised me.
Someplace we grew apart.
I went to another place
and never came back.

• • •

Inside, a voice told me to
walk as far as I
could at night without stopping.

The night was cold and low-lit
the men kept looking
asking if I was for sale.

I said no and they did not
make me do what the
other women were doing.

I put my head down and walked
away and into
the dark where the water roared.

There in the dark alley a
man on a woman
undulating away.

I looked at the water and cried.
The stars were bright and the
black waves rose and fell.

● ● ●

(For Wuendy Aguilar)

Their tired fingers are swollen from cutting
out squishy fishy entrails
delivered by disappearing boats
gliding on the freezing waves of the open sea.

Achy feet holding up their bodies;
their hands anchoring irritated fingers
bloodied red with orange hues
by open veins and castigating exoskeletons.

Burning the inside of the backs of these bodies.
Their blood pumps up and down their legs
through newly minted varicose veins
and swollen ankles
and bloated bellies from drinking too much beer,

shedding too many tears,
not having enough sex, way too much TV,
too many *semitas*, empanadas y plátanos[vi]
and cell phone exposure.

They disembowel bass
to keep up with the latest trends of SPAM.

• • •

We are the roaches hidden between your walls
outliving humans.
Sturdy colonies always grow larger,
living longer.

Stronger against the pesticides
they do not die in the fields
where your strawberries grow.

We should not die among your food.
We should stand outside your walls
and wait for you to let us in and out
when we are done with your yards
your chickens, your fish, and your children.

We are the new foxes in your forests.
You come in the night with your hounds
smelling us out trying to kill us.

We belong to the turtles
who know when to disappear
and when to rear their heads.

• • •

My Auntie: *Whatever you do, say nothing.*
My teacher: *Don't show people what you feel.*
My mentor: *I will give you an executive coach to check your face because I can't stand the way you look when you're thinking.*
My Latina mentor: *You are wasting your talents on these children.*
My clinical supervisor: *There is no place here at work for you to be who you are.*
My Latina lover: *I only care about your brain.*
My boss: *I'd like you to dress up more like me for work.*
My professor: *I'm not happy with how little you teach my students.*
My state police officer: *Where are you going? Where do you work? Can I see your work ID?*
My fellow Latina activist: *You are not part of my community.*
My fellow feminist activist: *You can't have it all you know, support this leader even though she is racist. She is a woman and that comes first.*

• • •

(For Wuendy Aguilar)

On my way home from work one night
arriving at the top of the T escalator
blue, white and red bright lights
with open doors waiting to swallow me whole.

Inside them, sitting
voices coming at us from all directions.
Within that sideways rain of sound,
a word I knew.

"*Papeles*".

Flooding images rushing through
of Uncle Isaías buying back my green card.
Uncle Isaías buying me a typewriter.
Uncle Isaías bringing me a fresh social security card.
"Type this number there."
"But isn't that illegal?"
"Everything should be illegal."

Brothers getting shot while crossing the Río.
Brothers learning M-16 lessons before knowing how to write
    their names.
Brothers buying pot with sex.
Brothers killing, molesting and raping.

MS[vii] taxi companies create jobs.
MS schools graduate alumns.
MS money buys plane tickets and guns.
MS brothers grow police and non-profit budgets
                        and make for good documentaries.

MS brothers selling guns for the cops.
MS brothers doing yard work.
MS brothers shoveling snow.
MS brothers justifying the jails.

We are Indian givers that keep on giving.

• • •

I don't know the difference
between the silence
after a rape
a beating
a break up
a shooting
a death
or after kneeling on corn kernels for misbehaving.

I don't know the difference
between the yearning for home
after an insult
a dirty look
a friend's betrayal
a humiliating doctor's visit
a burial
or good sex.

I cry through all of it.
My hands on my chest.

● ● ●

My sister texted me one day.
The text said "I love you."
I wrote back "Who is this?"
She wrote back "Your sister, Melissa."
I wrote back "You don't know me."
"I love you. We are family."
"I don't know you."
"I love you. We are family."
"I don't believe you."
"I am your sister."
"You are talking to my brother now, aren't you?"
"Yes. We have to forgive."
"Is she there?"
"Who?"
"Your mother."
"I'm an adult now."
"I want nothing to do with her."
"OK. We have to forgive."
"I see you are a Christian now."
"Yes. Jesus saved me."
"I will not be baptized."
"It is OK. We are family."
"Up to you."

● ● ● ●

I'm sorry but I can't go back where I come from.
I no longer speak that language.
I cannot make tortillas.
Grow beans.
Make tamales.
I go shopping at supermarkets.
Drive a car of my own.
I get jobs and make money.
I put food in the microwave.
I put my hands in women's pussies.

Buckets full of apples and squash.
The gray mornings when it's just a little too chilly.
The joy of sleeping in my bed.

The sweat under my wool sweater
after an afternoon hike with my dogs.
Steamy cider on my stove,
Loaves of bread,
Hot chilies and soups.

A good book.
Rainy days.
Sticky mud.
Puttering buds.
Brown stream beds swollen.

Those days when everything sticks.
Mosquitoes, flatworms, ticks.
The sun wraps around my skin.

● ● ● ●

We head to the mountain at dawn.

We slither
          through

    the silent
trees;

past the women
    carrying pails brimming with ground corn,
past the place
    where men walked with machetes in their hands,
past unbound boys
          running through the cornfields.

The girls are inside the
              worn

                    down

                          houses

They hide   the weight of the dishes, the laundry
under

and the men,
and the women.

              And the trees
        were their havens in the dark.

● ● ● ●

(For Mercedes Sosa)

In the morning, broken toenails
walk into the market on scraggly roads.
The women roll hundreds of thousands of dumplings
and bake them on pyres of iron
and wood and dirty jokes.

They whisper at the darkest point of night.
Their voices pierce the morning's blazing light.

Their holy baskets perched in front of
half empty market stalls.

Their singing in shrill voices while wiping mud on their dirty aprons.
"Tortillas, tortillas, tortillas!"
"¿Quiere tortillas mi amorcito?"[viii]

● ● ● ●

The son walked careful toward the sun
on a staircase of stories of old.
Under there, the daughter of another.

Moon Jaguar, consort of witches,
who spoke at length with snakes and jaguars,
made her from red clay and will and prayers.

Rosalila of the bright pinks, peaches and soft greens
lay hidden under layers of rock
to be found one day by naked eyes.

Rosalila of the soft curves
and walls of handprints
withstanding the passage of time.

● ● ● ●

Into the dark.
In it an abyss.
Feet and hands touching grass and dirt and rocks.
Eyes bound by the night.
Between hands and feet
the heartbeat drumming.
Breath accompanies.

Sounds of whispers and sighs,
prayers and yearnings,
made low and loud
reverberate.

● ● ● ●

They will rupture the shell
Mother has built around our bones.

They will see our faces
peeking into their New World.

New World meeting Old World.
Old World periled,
ossified,
excavated,
seen in their image:
Vesbian artifacts,[ix]
sons and daughters of Mitch.

Our eyes an imprint
on a plank of concrete
suggesting a time when we were in 3D.
We will be fragile,
ancient,
mysterious,
lost.

● ● ● ●

A man walks through the front door of my house with a sack of
    green bananas.
He's walked ten miles with the fifty pounds on his back.

Tío Abraham, is fifty, I think.
It is hard to tell how old he is.
His skin is copper brown.
Wrinkles don't show until you are really old
when you have copper brown skin.

I puff up my chest and bring out a smile.
I tell him I love the sack of bananas.
He tells me he picked them himself.
He wants to know about me.

The phone rings.
I get on the phone and I say "How are you dear?"
She says "Missing you my love."
I say "What have you been doing?"
She says "You know, busy."
I say "I miss you so much."
She says "You'll be here soon."
I say "I just needed to hear your voice."
She says "Me too. I love you."
I hang up.

He's still there. Smiling.
Wants to know who called.
I say a friend.

I don't want him to know about me.
How can I tell him about
nights of snowy January hikes
to the suburban house
from where I would surface at First Light?

• • • •

They call us *paleros*ˣ
and say we are evil.
We dance in the forests
and conjure up demons
to wreak havoc on peaceful homes,
steady marriages and
godly men.

When I feel like being evil,
I go to the trees.
The other day,
a spirit stood on a branch.
His face glowed big smiles.

I said "Grandfather,
can you knock some sense into the godly men?"

He looked at me.
"Child you are impatient."

• • • •

(For Dalila Dermith for daring to dream of a better world for all Hondurans despite their resentment of you)

They called you *mujer culebra*[xi]
as if they'd known Flamenco Beach.
Rocky cliffs overrun with tall *zacate*[xii],
shark infested waters, and
left over bombs from the U.S. target practices.

They meant your name an insult.
They did not know *culebras* to be
soothing serpentine *susurros susurrando*[xiii]
of the futures flanking us on all sides.

Your glory and your rage,
seething and seeding,
feeding.

● ● ● ●

El viento de tus sueños
suena fuerte en las ramas vacías
del invierno. Vuela terco
hacia el sol naciente.
Crece allí un poquito y se mueve
hacia el río fluctuante sureño.
En la corriente atorbellinada
se calienta y sube
discreto hacia el Pacífico.
En el lugar del ocaso se azulea
y se disipa en las entrañas
del Orión inquieto.[xiv]

A seed, under the sun
became a coin.
Under the *molcajete*[xv]
a spice.

Under the spell of Obatalá
dancing up and down
the mountain passes,
it meets the corn,
and the cloves,
and the wise old woman
with the one pound stone
that brings them together
into a full embrace.

The embrace crushes
and mixes and makes them into dust.
And the dust meets the milk,
and then the fire.

What is left is pinol,[xvi]
feeding the hungry belly.

In the heat of day
Yemayá you come to greet me
cooling my feet and neck
to welcome the moment.

This moment when I want to run
like a madwoman down the street
silently punching out whoever stands in my way.

In you, the oil, decaying bodies,
the trash and dead zones.
In you, the Blue whales still
talk, the dolphins and the sea turtles
still delight.
In you, algae stretches far into the upper place
and plankton shines at night.

Just when I think our world has run out,
you touch me tender and cold, and make me small.

Yemayá, keep me small
that I may see wonder,
so my heart may never shrink and dry out.

Spider Women weaving a web of pure delight.
Visions are the things you see and smell and touch in 3D.
The way each of your faces soften when you look at me,
your lingering smells after you leave each night,
Your mix of Lumbee fatback in my greens,
Southern Black Eyed Peas for New Year's Dinner,
Peking Duck and stir-fried bok choy,
Sofrito and pernil,
Barbeque'd ribs and other made-up food,
All the comfort and the safety of your embrace,
The ways in which we hold on to each other in the mornings.

Those maple syrup voices

and the multi-colored quilt that is your skin,
keeping me warm in winter,
giving me shelter under the dead heat.
And your minds,
blowing open every wall,
seeing and naming what lies beneath each word,
asking every question to be asked,
welcoming the arrival of every thought.

And then there are your children.
Furry and furless.

Children that feed others.

Children that have budgets and require buildings.
Children that already have other children.
Children of the streets and bordellos.

You hover about your task
and make each other laugh
while birthing worlds
that ripple throughout your webs
and into each other.

I am the one that unleashed your rivers.
Earn my trust by getting dirty,
by dipping your heart into water.
Soak all of you for a while.
Then I will hold your nipples between my fingers.

You floated naked with the ebbing flowing current.
I lost myself in your folds of skin.

I made you putty in my hands.
I rose above you.
Made you small.
Rolled you into a little ball.
I stretched you until you burned.

I pressed you down and held you steady.

I made you *masa* under my stone.
I made you thick and thin.
Wet and dry.

The subtle curves in your mane
Make me want to grab them tightly.

I take you and make you senseless
day after day
Woman of the Butterfly Clan.

Long lineages
of unwed mothers,
prostitutes, victims, addicts,
warriors, priestesses and wizards,
alcoholics, rapists, molesters,
murderers, dead beat dads and dead ones
run through our bodies.

Yet, you shine brighter than all others
in this moment
when I make you mine.
You are the work of your choices
bright-eyed, lying naked
underneath me.

Woman you are Vulture,
connected to the rising heat
swirling under hungry hawks
up above tree lines
lining up highways
towering into the clouds.

Woman you are Jaguar
leaping across the world
and space towards Orion,
Xibalba rising,
bringing our prayers,
bringing back our answers.
You harbor our dreams.
You sneak in our visions.
You sculpt our worlds into being.

Woman you are the Corn
crushed under the weight of our bodies.
Our teeth make you unrecognizable.
Our bellies render you a liquid.
Our blood sucks you dry.
Our brains make you sing.
Our hands give you purpose and shape.
Our eyes speckle your color.
Our tongues writhing.

Woman you are Butterfly
flapping about from place to place
touching lightly
on your landing pads,
launching smoothly
as if taking a walk on a Sunday afternoon
when it's sunny outside
and warm
and mosquito-free.

In the vastness of the new day
I long for you *y me apuro*[xvii]
through the hours in a frenzied countdown.
Al fin[xviii], I dive into you.

In your eyes, I am a fertile reef.
In your hands, my heart is *barro rojo*[xix].
In my eyes, you are hibiscus in bloom.
In my hands, *sos azul y verde*[xx] as a swollen berth.
I drop my anchor there, in the depth of your *querer*[xxi].

Laughter ebbs and flows.
My cheeks hurt at the end of dinner from laughing.

With you, my day ends as purple as the setting sun.

[i] From the Maya baálamk'aan: the place of jaguars and snakes
[ii] and the children become | men, and women, | full of water and the men and women | flow with the Chamelecón River | and it suffices
[iii] She went to wait for me.
[iv] Slated windows
[v] Cornfields
[vi] Sweet bread, fritters and plantains.
[vii] MS-13 gang
[viii] "Want tortillas my darling Love?"
[ix] From Vesubius
[x] Palero: Practitioner of one of the three gateways of Santeria. Literally means "he of the sticks".
[xi] Snake Woman
[xii] Grass
[xiii] Whispers whispering
[xiv]

The wind in your dreams
sounds loud on the empty branches
of winter. It flies stubbornly
towards the rising sun.
It grows there a little y it moves towards
the southern flowing river.
Within the river's tumultuous current
it heats up and rises
discreetly towards the Pacific.
In that place where sunset takes place it turns blue
and it dissipates in the entrails
of a ramped up Orion.

[xv] Mortar and pestle
[xvi] Pinol: a hot or cold drink made of the mixture of pulverized cocoa and corn kernels. Usually made and consumed by indigenous people from Central America.
[xvii] And I hurry
[xviii] At last
[xix] Red clay
[xx] You are blue and green
[xxi] Longing

www.ingramcontent.com/pod-product-compliance
Lightning Source LLC
LaVergne TN
LVHW091319080426
835510LV00007B/566